BRITAIN IN WORLD WAR II

Women's War

Alison Cooper

Based on an original text by
Fiona Reynoldson

an imprint of Hodder Children's Books

BRITAIN IN WORLD WAR II
Titles in this series
THE BLITZ
EVACUATION
RATIONING
WOMEN'S WAR

Original design: Nick Cannan
Differentiated design: Raynor Design
This title designed by: Joy Mutter
Text consultant: Norah Granger

Based on an original text *The Home Front – Women's War*, by Fiona Reynoldson, published in 1991 by Wayland Publishers Ltd

This edition published in 2003 by Hodder Wayland, an imprint of Hodder Children's Books

British Library Cataloguing in Publication Data
Cooper, Alison, 1967 - Women's war. - Differentiated ed. - (Britain in World War II)
1. World War, 1939-1945 - Women - Great Britain - Juvenile literature 2. Great Britain - Social conditions - 20th century - Juvenile literature I. Title II. Reynoldson, Fiona 941'.084

ISBN 0 7502 4307 4

Printed and bound by G. Canale & C. S.p.A. - Borgaro T.se - Turin

Hodder Children's Books
a division of Hodder Headline Limited
338 Euston Road, London NW1 3BH

 See page 31 for ways in which you can use this book to encourage literacy skills.

Acknowledgements
The publishers would like to thank HarperCollins Publishers Ltd for permission to quote from *Women Who Went to War* © 1988 Eric Taylor. Copyright in the customised version vests in Hodder & Stoughton Ltd.

The publishers would like to thank the following for permission to reproduce their pictures: ET Archive 7 (top), 15 (left); Hulton-Deutsch 5; The Trustees of the Imperial War Museum 7 (bottom), 8 (bottom), 10, 11 (left), 12, 13 (bottom), 14, 15 (right), 16, 18, 19, 20, 21, 22, 23 (top), 24 (top), 29 (bottom); Peter Newark's Military Pictures 4, 8 (top), 11 (right), 17, 23 (bottom); Topham Picture Library 6, 9 (top), 13 (top), 24 (bottom), 26, 27, 28, 29 (top). The map on page 25 was drawn by Peter Bull. Cover image: supplied by Hulton Archive, 'Fire Training' reference HL5189.

Contents

Women's Work

During the First World War of 1914-1918, many men left their everyday jobs. They became sailors, soldiers or airmen instead. Women took over some of the jobs the men had done.

► This poster asks women to come and work in factories making munitions – ammunition for guns.

◄ These women are making biscuits in a factory in Liverpool in 1926.

Women drove buses and worked on farms. They worked in factories making ammunition for guns. They helped to keep the country going. People were used to women working as servants or nurses. Now they realized that women could do 'men's work' too – even the really tough, dirty jobs.

When the First World War ended, the men came home. They needed their old jobs back. Women stopped doing 'men's work'. Instead, they worked in shops or offices, or in factories making food or clothes. Some worked as teachers or doctors. Many women did not go out to work at all after they got married.

The War Begins

The Second World War began in 1939. One of the first big changes was evacuation. The government thought that German aeroplanes would drop bombs on big cities as soon as the war started. They decided to move children and mothers with babies to safer areas of the country.

► These children are leaving home for a safer place in the country.

◀ Here, shops and houses have been blown up by bombs but people still have to do their shopping.

Only babies and toddlers were evacuated with their mothers. Older children travelled with their classmates and teachers. They went to live with families in the countryside.

▼ A young girl being rescued from a bombed house.

Some evacuees enjoyed their new life in the country but others were miserable. Many children were unhappy at being away from their families. No bombs fell on the cities at the start of the war, so many evacuees went home.

Later, when the cities were bombed, many mothers decided to keep their children with them. One mother said, 'I'm blowed if I'd let my kids go again.'

On the Farm

This is a government poster asking women to join the Land Army.

▶ These women are sawing logs to make pit props. These were needed to hold up the roofs of the tunnels in coal-mines.

During the Second World War, women were again needed to work on the land and in factories because men had joined the armed forces. Britain had to produce more food than ever during the war because German submarines were sinking ships bringing food from other countries. The government asked women to join the Women's Land Army and go to work on farms.

In August 1940 the Women's Land Army had only 7,000 members, but by 1943 the number had risen to 77,000. Land Army members did all sorts of jobs. They milked cows, picked vegetables, cleared ditches and cut down trees.

Life in the Land Army could be tough. Women had to work long hours, even in bad weather. Sometimes they did not have very comfortable places to live in.

▲ These Land Army women are bringing in the harvest on a farm in Suffolk.

Although it was hard work, a lot of women enjoyed the healthy life in the countryside. Young women had more freedom than they would have had at home with their parents.

One woman described how at harvest time she 'worked with a gang of four girls going round Wiltshire farms with a steam-engine and threshing tackle'.

Factory Work

Thousands of women went to work in factories. They made equipment that Britain needed to fight the war, such as aircraft parts or ammunition.

Some women were worried that they would not do such a good job as the men. Most soon found they had nothing to worry about. One woman said, 'We were working from drawings to make the very first Lancaster [an aircraft] and I was amazed how many men couldn't understand a drawing. I could.'

► These women are making fuses for shells.

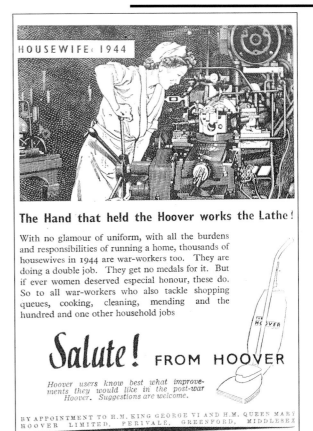

▲ Mothers shared the job of looking after children, so that more women could go to work in the factories.

▲ Goods like vacuum cleaners were not on sale during the war. Companies put adverts like this in the newspapers so that people would not forget about them.

Even if women factory workers were very good at their jobs, they never earned the same as men. In one aircraft factory women were paid 43 shillings a week (£2.15) but men were paid 73 shillings (£3.65) for doing exactly the same job. In 1943 the women went on strike. They got a pay rise – but it was still not as much as the men's wage.

Volunteers

Farm work and factory work were very important but other work had to be done as well. Women worked in shops, banks and offices. Married women had housework to do and children to look after. Chores like shopping took longer than usual because there were often queues at food shops.

Many women who could not do war work full time joined the Women's Voluntary Service (WVS). By 1944 the WVS had one million members.

▼ Workers enjoying a cup of tea at a WVS mobile canteen.

The WVS did all sorts of jobs. In the cities they set up rest centres for people whose homes had been bombed. They set up mobile canteens too, so that people could get a meal. They drove ambulances. WVS members were all volunteers, which means they did not get paid for doing any of these jobs.

Outside the cities the WVS ran nurseries for working mothers and looked after evacuees. One woman remembered 'sitting with other women knitting seamen's stockings, while the small children played with the balls of wool'.

▲ Women spent a lot of time queuing for food.

▼ These WVS members are handing out clothes to people whose homes have been bombed.

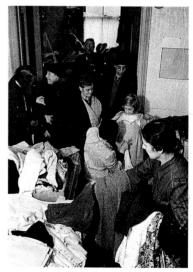

The Blitz

In 1940, about a year after the war started, German aeroplanes began to bomb British cities. These attacks were known as 'the Blitz'. London was the first city to be attacked. Night after night, people went to air-raid shelters for protection from the bombing.

Many women worked as air-raid wardens. Barbara Nixon was an air-raid warden. She cycled to each of the public shelters in her area, checking that everyone was all right. Once, she was blown right off her bicycle by the blast from a bomb. If houses were hit, she called in the fire service and ambulances. She helped to rescue anyone trapped in the rubble.

► These women are using powerful searchlights to try to spot enemy bombers.

▲ These people are sheltering in a London Underground station.

▲ An air-raid warden ready for work.

Some members of the Women's Royal Naval Service (WRNS – sometimes known as 'Wrens') worked in the Special Minewatch Units. During an air-raid they kept watch along the River Thames. If they saw enemy aeroplanes drop mines in the water, the river had to be closed. The mines had to be cleared before ships could use the river.

Life in the ATS

Women were not allowed to fight the enemy directly but they were able to join the women's branches of the army, navy and air force. The women's branch of the army was called the Auxiliary Territorial Service (ATS). By July 1942 it had 217,000 members.

Some women did not enjoy life in the ATS very much. One woman described how 'we'd run and run and march long routes, with packs on our backs and blisters on our heels.'

▶ These ATS cooks are learning how to prepare a meal on an outdoor stove.

The ATS did a wide range of jobs. Many women worked as cooks, cleaners or clerks. Others drove trucks or worked as electricians, carpenters or welders. They operated searchlights and even worked on gun sites. They targeted enemy aircraft and loaded the guns, but they were not allowed to fire them.

▼ An ATS member shouting orders on a gun site.

▼ The prime minister, Winston Churchill, said this poster made the ATS look too glamorous. He stopped it from being used.

Women in the Air Force

The WAAF was the Women's Auxiliary Air Force. Sometimes, women joined the WAAF because they thought it would be very exciting. Often, they found themselves doing the same work as women in the other services – cooking and office jobs.

Some WAAFs worked in operations rooms. They marked the movements of British and enemy aircraft on big maps. Others repaired and maintained the aircraft. Only women in the ATA (see pages 20–21) were allowed to fly.

▼ WAAF mechanics repairing a Wellington bomber.

▲ A WAAF electrician working on a Lancaster bomber in 1943.

▲ A nurse from the Royal Air Force (RAF) nursing service receives a patient. The army, navy and air force each had their own nurses.

One WAAF mechanic remembered a time when she did take off – unexpectedly! It was part of her job to sit on the tailplane of the Spitfires as they rolled to the runway. One day a pilot forgot to stop and let her jump off: 'I just lay flat down across the tail unit and clung on,' she said. Luckily for her, the pilot quickly made a perfect landing.

High Fliers

The only women pilots belonged to the Air Transport Auxiliary (ATA) and they had all learned to fly before the war. Their job was to fly aeroplanes from the factories where they were made to the airfields where they were needed. At first only eight of the ATA's pilots were women but eventually the number grew to 120.

▼ The woman on the left is an ATA flying instructor. The man is a trainee pilot.

▲ ATA women pilots in their flying suits.

The first women pilots were only allowed to fly Tiger Moths. These were old aeroplanes with open cockpits. Later, they learned to fly fifteen different types of aeroplane.

Some of the aeroplanes were so new that their radios had not been fitted. The women could not get instructions from controllers on the ground. They used maps, compasses and their view of the ground below to help them find their way.

▲ A Polish woman pilot who came to Britain and joined the ATA.

Work Behind the Scenes

Radar is a way of finding out where ships and aeroplanes are, before you can actually see them. Women worked at radar stations all around the coast of Britain. They looked for enemy aeroplanes or ships on their radar screens. Then they passed the information to gunners on the ground or pilots in the air to help them find the enemy.

▼ ATS members mark the position of enemy ships in the English Channel on a map.

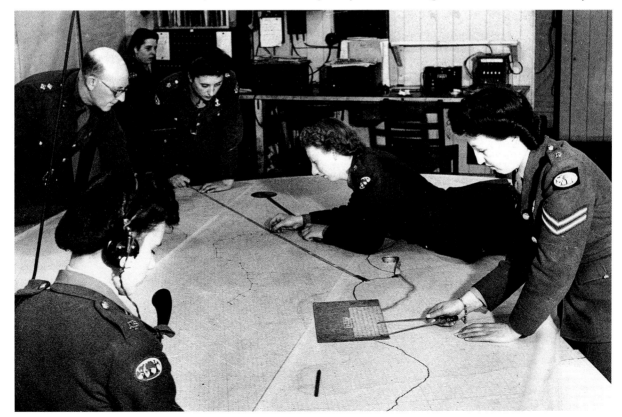

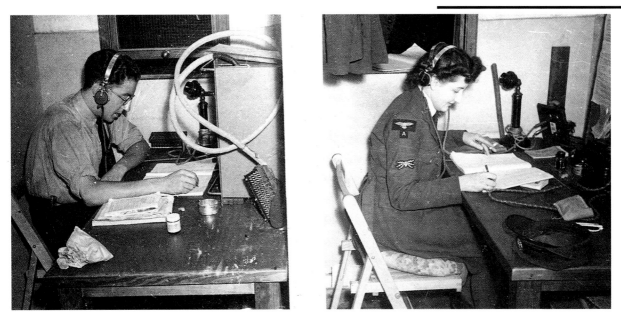

▲ Radio operators taking messages from British pilots in 1942. ▲

During wartime important messages are sent in secret codes. The Germans used a machine called Enigma to put their messages into code. They thought the Enigma codes were so complicated no one would ever be able to work out what they meant.

This poster warns people that enemy spies might be listening to them.

The British used early types of computer to work out what the German messages meant. They even had some captured Enigma machines to help them. About 2,000 women did top-secret work as code-breakers. One woman described the big, rattling computers they used: 'We were standing up most of the time . . . the noise was awful.'

Lives in Danger

▲ Violette Szabo was a secret agent. She was caught by the Germans and shot.

Some women did very dangerous work during the Second World War. They worked as secret agents for the Allies in countries that were occupied by the enemy.

One woman, Phyllis Latour, was dropped by parachute into France. She found out what sort of defences the Germans had built along the French coast. She sent the information back to Britain in coded messages. This helped the Allies, who were planning to invade France and push the Germans out.

► Odette Churchill (centre) was a secret agent too, but she was lucky enough to survive the war. She and Violette Szabo were both awarded medals for bravery.

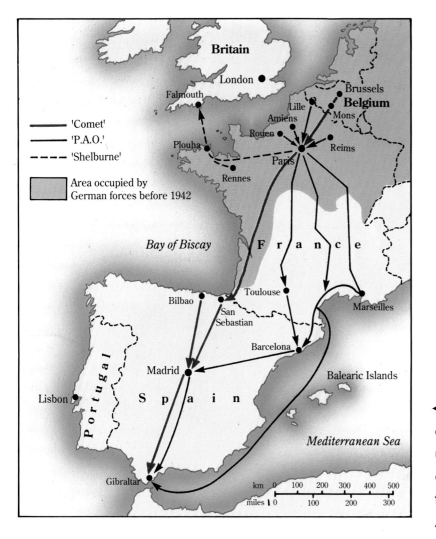

'Comet'

'P.A.O.'

'Shelburne'

Area occupied by
German forces before 1942

◀ This map shows three of the escape routes set up to help Allied pilots to escape. The Comet route from Brussels was run by Andrée de Jongh.

Helping pilots who had been shot down was another dangerous job. One Belgian woman called Andrée de Jongh ran an escape route. Pilots were moved from one hiding place to another. Eventually, they reached safety in Spain.

Women who did this kind of work knew they might be captured by the Germans. Those who were captured were imprisoned. Many were shot, or died in prison camps.

Keeping Cheerful

It was often hard to feel cheerful during wartime. Families were separated and people did not know if they would ever see their loved ones again. Songs like this one sung by Vera Lynn encouraged people to be brave:

We'll meet again
Don't know where, don't know when
But I know we'll meet again
Some sunny day.

▼ These soldiers are coming home on leave. They are waving to their families who are waiting for them at the station.

At the end of 1941, the USA joined Britain in the war against Germany. This news made people in Britain feel more cheerful.

▲ The singer Ann Shelton making a radio programme to entertain British soldiers in India.

Soon, American soldiers arrived in Britain. One woman said 'The American soldiers were so glamorous and they had plenty of money.' By May 1944, 20,000 British women had married American soldiers. People wanted to plan for the future, even though they did not know when the war would end.

Home Again

The war in Europe ended in May 1945. The Allies had defeated the Germans. Victory parties were held all over Britain.

There were 460,000 women in services like the WAAF and the ATS when the war ended. Another six and a half million women were doing jobs such as working in factories or on farms. Now their war work was over, as one ATS member explained: 'I saw my name on a list and suddenly realized my days in the ATS were fast coming to an end. I was told to hand in my kit at the stores. I was out, services no longer required.'

► These women are dancing in the street to celebrate the end of the war.

◄ A soldier is welcomed home by his family.

◄ These Wrens guided boats up the River Thames. Many women thought their wartime jobs were more exciting than running a home.

Some women missed their war work and the friends they had made. One woman said: 'The war was over. Back to the home. I found the next few years very hard.' Others were just relieved to get back to normal life. As one Glasgow woman said: 'No more bombs. We all looked forward to the future.'

Glossary

Allies The countries that fought together in the Second World War against Germany and Japan. The main Allies were Britain, the Soviet Union and the USA.

ammunition Bullets or shells (see below) that are fired from guns.

cockpit The part of an aeroplane where the pilot sits and controls the plane.

compass A dial with an arrow that always points to the north.

evacuee A person who has been evacuated – moved from a dangerous area to a safer one.

fuse A fuse is the part of a shell (see below) that has to be lit to make it explode.

mine A bomb that is designed to float in water and explode if a boat passes over it.

parachute A large piece of fabric attached to a harness. It opens up when a person jumps out of an aeroplane and allows him/her to float slowly to the ground.

radar A system that uses radio waves to find objects that are too far away to be seen.

shell A shell is like a large bullet, packed with explosives and fired from a large gun.

submarine A ship that is designed to travel under water.

threshing tackle Machinery used to separate the grains of wheat and other cereals from the stalks after they have been harvested.

Wrens Members of the Women's Royal Naval Service (WRNS).

Projects

1. Ask if any women in your family did war work. What did they do? Did they have to move away from home? Did they enjoy it?

2. Which of the jobs described in this book would you like to have done? Which job wouldn't you like to have done? Why?

Books to Read

The Diary of a Young Nurse in World War II by Moira Butterfield (Watts, 2001)

The History Detective Investigates Women's War by Martyn Parsons (Hodder Wayland, 2000)

Women's War by Stewart Ross (Evans, 2002)

Places to Visit

Eden Camp, Malton, North Yorkshire YO17 6RT. Tel: 01653 697777.
This museum is based in an old army camp. It tells you about everyday life in the Second World War.

Imperial War Museum, Lambeth Road, London SE1 6HZ.
Tel: 0207 416 5320.
This museum covers all aspects of life in the Second World War.

Winston Churchill's Britain at War Experience, 64-66 Tooley St, London Bridge, London SE1 2TF. Tel: 0207 403 3171.
In this museum you can find out what it was like to live through an air raid or to be evacuated, and there is also information about the Land Army and other wartime jobs done by women.

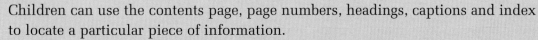

Use this book for teaching literacy

This book can help you in the literacy hour in the following ways:

✓ Children can use the contents page, page numbers, headings, captions and index to locate a particular piece of information.

✓ Posters, advertisements and newspaper headlines are good examples of the different styles of writing needed for Year 4 literacy teaching.

✓ Children can use the glossary to reinforce their alphabetic knowledge and extend their vocabulary.

✓ They can compare this book with fictional stories about World War II and women's role in it, to show how similar information can be presented in different ways.

Index

Numbers in **bold** refer to pictures and captions.